www.iCharacter.org
Published by iCharacter Ltd. (Ireland)
By Agnes de Bezenac
Illustrated by Agnes de Bezenac
Colored by Jackson
Copyright 2019. All rights reserved.

Copyright © 2019 by iCharacter Limited. All rights reserved. No part of this book may be reproduced in any form or by any electronic or mechanical means, including information storage and retrieval systems, without written permission from the publisher or author, except in the case of a reviewer, who may quote brief passages embodied in critical articles or in a review.

Noah

He says...

Work well

He says...

Be gentle

He says...

Pray always

He says...

Be patient

Samson

He says...

Be strong

Joseph

He says...

Forgive

Queen Esther

She says...

Be brave

He says...

Be wise

Samuel

Moses

Jonah

He says...

Obey

He says...

Be clean

He says...

Learn

She says...

Be still

Paul

He says...

Be bold

He says...

Trust

Mary Madgelene

He says...

I love you

More books from iCharacter.org

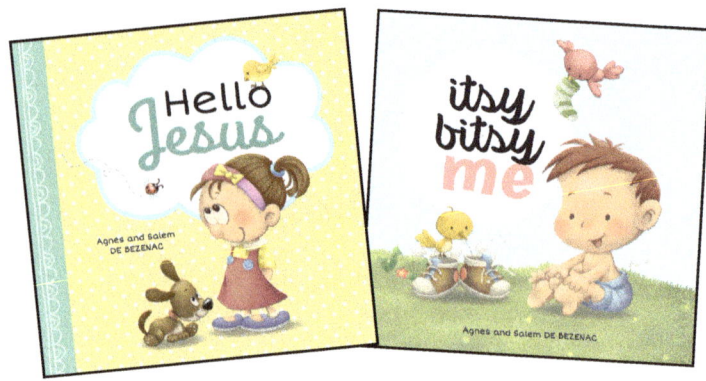

www.ingramcontent.com/pod-product-compliance
Lightning Source LLC
Chambersburg PA
CBHW061811070526
44586CB00024B/2801